WE
THE PEOPLE
FRANCIS MARION

Published by Creative Education, Inc. 123 South
Broad Street, Mankato, Minnesota 56001

Library of Congress Cataloging-in-Publication Data

Zadra, Dan.
  Francis Marion: swamp fox, 1732-1795.

  (We the people)
  Summary: A brief biography of the southern
plantation owner and general whose knowledge of the
swamps helped keep the Revolution alive in the South.
  1. Marion, Francis, 1732-1795—Juvenile literature.
2. Generals—United States—Biography—Juvenile
literature.   3. South Carolina—Militia—Biography—
Juvenile literature.   4. United States—History—
Revolution, 1775-1783—Juvenile literature.
[1. Marion, Francis, 1732-1795.   2. Generals.
3. United States—History—Revolution, 1775-1783—
Biography]   I. Keely, John, ill.   II. Brude, Dick, ill.
III. Title.   IV. Series.
E207.M3Z33   1988   973.3'3'0924 [B] [92]   87-36387
ISBN 0-88682-196-7

WE
THE PEOPLE
FRANCIS MARION

SWAMP FOX
(1732-1795)

DAN ZADRA

Illustrated By John Keely and Dick Brude

CREATIVE EDUCATION

FRANCIS MARION

The true story of Francis Marion, the fabled "Swamp Fox," begins in old South Carolina. There, in 1732, a sixth child was born to the Marion family of Goatfield Plantation. He was so tiny and frail. "Hardly bigger than a lobster," his father said. "We'll call him Francis."

Little Francis was a constant source of worry to his parents. He was often sick, and he grew much slower than the other children. But he was a quick-witted boy, full of spirit as a bantam rooster. If there was a tree no one dared to climb, Francis would climb it. If there was a horse no one else could ride, Francis would ride it.

Often, he would go alone into the swamps that surrounded the plantation. While his mother wrung her hands in worry, Francis would hunt, fish or just watch the birds and animals. And he never got lost.

When he was 15, Francis told his parents he wanted to become a sailor. There was no stopping him once his mind was made up. So, off he went to the wild West Indies.

His schooner ran into a whale and sank. Francis and the other crewmen were cast adrift in an open boat for seven days. Some of the strong men died—but not weak Francis. He and the other survivors were finally rescued. Francis came home looking healthier than ever. Danger seemed to agree with him!

He decided to give up the sea and help his parents with the plantation. Unlike other "gentlemen farmers," Francis rolled up his sleeves and worked right alongside the field slaves and hirelings. As the years passed, his body grew rock-hard and strong. Little Francis was frail no more.

In those days, South Carolina

was a royal colony ruled by King George of England. But the French wanted to take over American lands. They urged the Indians to rise up against the settlers. Soon, fierce Cherokee warriors attacked the colonists in South Carolina.

Naturally, Francis Marion joined the militia. He took part in the campaign that forced the Indians to make a peace treaty.

After the Cherokee War, Francis went back to farming. He prospered, and in 1773 he bought Pond Bluff, a large plantation on the Santee River. With the help of black slaves, he grew tobacco, corn, and other crops.

The days were long and the work was mighty hard. So whenever he could, Francis slipped away to enjoy the eerie peace of his beloved swamps. He would glide along silently in a boat beneath the moss-hung cypress trees, fishing and thinking. Oh, how he loved this wet and mysterious land. "The day is coming," thought Francis sadly, "when I may have to give my life to protect it."

There was talk of another war. For many years, American colonists had labored under British rule and taxes. Most of the people of South Carolina — including Francis Marion—wanted liberty. In 1775 the colonists finally rebelled.

Francis represented the people of South Carolina in the Provincial Congress, which adopted the Bill of Rights. Then he was commissioned a captain in the small colonial army. A

shrewd and fearless leader, Francis was quickly promoted to major. His fierce South Carolina volunteers helped drive British troops out of Charleston, the most important seaport.

In June, 1776, British warships

tried to re-take the city. Marion and his men fought them in the Battle of Fort Moultrie. By now, he had risen to the rank of lieutenant colonel. Using captured cannons, Colonel Marion and the colonists drove the British ships away. On July 4, 1776, America officially declared its independence from Britain.

After a glorious start, the Revolu-

tionary War in the South fizzled out. The British installed a powerful army of experienced redcoats at Savannah. The small and poorly-equipped American force did not dare attack. For several years, the frustrated colonial troops could do nothing but watch and wait. Troop morale sunk lower and lower. But tough little Francis Marion would not let his men

go to pieces. They did not have fancy uniforms or proper equipment. But he kept them alert and ready to fight.

Finally, in 1779, the American forces tried to take Savannah from the British. But they were badly defeated. The survivors were put under the command of Francis Marion. He now became the senior field officer in South Carolina.

Meanwhile, the British were scheming to crush the Americans, once and for all. The plan was to send a giant army under Lord Cornwallis, to invade the colonial strongholds in South Carolina. The plan nearly worked. General Cornwallis took Charleston and captured most of the American officers. Francis Marion was able to escape, but Cornwallis

wasn't worried. What could one American do against so many British?

Next, Cornwallis and his army swung into Camden, S.C. and overran an American defense led by General Gates. It looked like the Revolutionary War in the South was lost.

But, wait! Francis Marion was

still at large. With just 30 hand-pick-
ed men, he snuck up on the British
and managed to free 150 American
prisoners. Then he and his men dis-
appeared into the dark Pee Dee River
swamps.

The British chased him but their
horses sank into the slimy ooze.
"We'll never find that cursed Swamp
Fox," roared the British commander.

Without knowing it, he had given Francis Marion a new name.

The "Swamp Fox" became a guerilla fighter. He set up his camp on Snow's Island, deep in the Pee Dee marshlands. From there, his small forces ranged out to attack British supply lines. His own men suffered from hunger and malaria. But they also spread terror among the British army. The people of South Carolina still yearned for liberty—and the Swamp Fox gave them new hope. Now a steady stream of men began to flow up the Pee Dee River to join the guerilla army.

But many colonists were still loyal to the British cause. General Cornwallis celebrated when he heard that a large loyalist force was march-

ing to join his British regulars. But the loyalists were met by Americans and defeated at the Battle of King's Mountain in October, 1780. The British lost their advantage.

Now General Nathanael Greene commanded American forces in the South. He sent word through the swamp, ordering Marion to attack

Georgetown, on the coast.

Marion had two forces. He ordered Colonel "Light-Horse" Harry Lee to attack with cavalry. The Swamp Fox himself brought the other force down the Pee Dee in boats. Together, they struck the British savagely. Without heavy guns, Marion's men couldn't break

the walls of the fort. But they did prevent British troops from leaving Georgetown. This meant that the main army of General Cornwallis was now stranded up North.

Part of that army suffered a great defeat at Cowpens. Then the angry British chased the American army into North Carolina, where Cornwallis fought Greene at Guilford Courthouse in March, 1781. As the battle raged on, the Swamp Fox moved in to cut British supply lines. He also attacked British and loyalist troops still in South Carolina. As usual, Marion had only a small, poorly-armed force. But his men were gritty and experienced. They took Fort Watson. Then they took Fort Motte by means of fire arrows! On May 29, 1781, they stormed into Georgetown and took it, too. The British had fled when they heard the Swamp Fox was coming!

Now, the Revolutionary War

swiftly drew to a close. In Virginia, Washington's army closed in on Cornwallis.

In South Carolina, Marion and General Greene defeated the last large British force at the Battle of Eutaw Springs. This occurred in August. In October, Cornwallis surrendered to the Americans after the Battle of Yorktown. The wily old

Swamp Fox rejoiced. Peace had come at last!

In August, 1782, Francis Marion went home to his plantation. It had been damaged during the war, so he rolled up his sleeves and repaired it. He married Mary Videau, and they settled down to a life of peace. But the legend of the feisty Swamp Fox lived on in stories and songs.

Many honors were given to him. He served in the senate and finally saw South Carolina become the eighth state of the Union in 1788. His last years, until his death in 1795, were spent near the beautiful and mysterious swamp country he had loved.

WE THE PEOPLE SERIES

WOMEN OF AMERICA

CLARA BARTON
JANE ADDAMS
ELIZABETH BLACKWELL
HARRIET TUBMAN
SUSAN B. ANTHONY
DOLLEY MADISON

INDIANS OF AMERICA

GERONIMO
CRAZY HORSE
CHIEF JOSEPH
PONTIAC
SQUANTO
OSCEOLA

FRONTIERSMEN OF AMERICA

DANIEL BOONE
BUFFALO BILL
JIM BRIDGER
FRANCIS MARION
DAVY CROCKETT
KIT CARSON

WAR HEROES OF AMERICA

JOHN PAUL JONES
PAUL REVERE
ROBERT E. LEE
ULYSSES S. GRANT
SAM HOUSTON
LAFAYETTE

EXPLORERS OF AMERICA

COLUMBUS
LEIF ERICSON
DeSOTO
LEWIS AND CLARK
CHAMPLAIN
CORONADO